National Poetry Series

Winner of the 1994

a hummock in

Matthew Rohrer   P o e m s

the malookas

New York London

W. W. Norton & Company

The text of this book is composed in Matrix Book,
with the display set in Mex.
Composed by Crane Typesetting Service, Inc.
Manufacturing by The Courier Companies, Inc.
Book design by Chris Welch

Library of Congress Cataloging-in-Publication Data
Rohrer, Mathew.
    A hummock in the Malookas : poems / Mathew Rohrer.
        p.   cm.
    "Winner of the 1994 national poetry series."
    I. Title
    PS3568.O52H86   1995
    811'.54—dc20   95-1729

ISBN 0-393-03798-3
W. W. Norton & Company, Inc., 500 Fifth Avenue, New York, N.Y. 10110
W. W. Norton & Company Ltd., 10 Coptic Street, London WC1A 1PU
1 2 3 4 5 6 7 8 9 0

For Susan

Contents

Two

Many thanks to the following journals in which some of these poems first appeared:

The Ajax Poetry Newsletter, The Cream City Review, Asylum Annual, Spirit, 100 Words, CutBank, The Denver Quarterly, The Iowa Review, and The Southern Poetry Review.

Thanks also to Jim Galvin, Marvin Bell, David Hamilton, and Lance Phillips, for their help and support.

"An unbearable thought I had in a working-class pub in Brussels: the mouldings on a door seemed to be endowed with a mysterious life of their own, and I remained in contact with their reality for a long time."

—René Magritte

venus waning/apollo waxing his car

Then there was the night I decided that if I ignored everyone
I would transcend,

so I covered my ears with my hands,
stepped off the porch and rose like a wet crow

and the sprinklers chattered to each other over the fences.
And "How long will you be gone?" my neighbor called nervously,
my neighbor whose saw I had borrowed,
and "Come down right now!" my landlord called out,
climbing to the roof of his Cadillac to reach me
as he got smaller and smaller.

And there I was with the stars hanging above my house like live wires
and the night sky the color of stockings.

I stuck out my tongue to taste the sky
but could not taste.

I inhaled deeply
but could not smell.

I used to look to the sky for comfort
and now there was nothing, not even a seam,
and I looked down and saw that it did not even reach the ground.

And my only company was the satellites counting in their sleep
and the Sorrowful Mother swinging her empty dipper in the darkness,
the Sorrowful Mother picking her way through the stars over my roof.

And I knew I was nowhere and if I ever took my hands from my ears
    I would fall.

the evening concert

There is a moment early in the evening
when everything seems possible.

An old man sits on a porch
eating,

telling you about sitting
on a porch eating.

Routine alone keeps an old man alive
on the first days of another spring.

Who knows what will happen next?
Then they hang the leaves back on the trees.

Everyone is on the edge of their seats
as the sun snuffs itself out

and the moment is over. It is night,
there are bats squeezed behind the shutters.

In the distance a car drives off the dock.
The cry of men running to help lifts up, a song.

the world just before the at ease

The violin in the pawnshop says,
I will never laugh if the gun tells a joke.

The statue of the maid with her vast bent back:
you hang wreaths on her in spring.

A child who is stung by twelve wasps
will have a better understanding of time

and a child who speaks kindly to an iridescent hornet
which stings him later by the lake says,
Now I have a better understanding of time.

The old stone tower that rises above the red-tiled roofs
is disappointed to discover that the sky it has admired all along
is colored by the lights in the parking lot.

The dark slits in the side of the tower are there
to remind you of history.

The river stumbles out of the forest and moves through the city
with its eyes closed.

You think the grass would taste sweet,
that a fox is humming while it inches through the shade.

The truth is, the dirt is spotless,
the river has a migraine,
the waiters are ashamed to serve anyone.

The truth is, when you're alone your bed is smaller,
and you are a bird with a sense of tragedy,
a bird in a room with a fever.

inside the egg something is laughing

A bird in a room with a fever
on a tiny bed made from a box of knives.

In the corner a girl fumbles with a match,
trying to heat a pan of water.
Her breath descends like a veil onto the stone floor.
Outside, the icy mountains loom.

Voices can be heard from below, angry voices,
dishes that have no choice in the matter yelling at each other
as they shatter against the bruising cupboards.

Somebody in the room whimpers; the girl cannot light a match.
Her brother is outside prying the frozen animals
from the side of the house
where they huddled for warmth.
It sounds like the bones of old trees snapping.

The only light in the room comes from a luminous fork.
The bird murmurs something from a dream. The girl cannot
light a match. The girl's pan has given up and gone to sleep.

In a rare moment of lucidity, the bird asks for a rope.
The bird asks to be shown the rapids where it once fed
on trout. It asks if it will be forgiven for dining on a creature
returning to its mother, to bring her flowers.
The girl cannot light a match. The luminous fork is so old
but remembers being forgotten by young people.

The girl has never seen a fork cry before
and she tries to catch its tear in her locket:
whose picture is this in here?

after the performance

After a mad and impassioned dance the evil magician is dead
and we stroll home over the untroubled bridge
festooned with lovers and curing carcasses.
It is June, the month renowned for love.
Shallow boats will tie up under the bridge to catch the carcasses
when they are cut down and fall into the river.

Barbaric, you say. On the other hand, I have forgotten the shock
of the first night I saw them: I thought they were hanged men,
I thought they were jeweled
because of the fireflies clinging to them.
Now you understand my use of the word "festooned."
I was drunk and it did not seem strange to me
that they would hang men off the bridge in their finery.

So you see a side of beef with luminous flies is a relief
to the drunken.
You say you are concerned that I drink too much without you,
and I say I raise my glass to the lovers on the bridge.
I raise my glass to the shallow boats and their open arms.
I raise my glass to the beautiful and distracting performances
    they put on for us in June.

the bridge

sleeps strung-out across the river
each morning. Gypsies have hung
nets and lures from its belly,
have peeled the shellfish from its arms.

The bridge crawls into town to drink at night.
Farms slumber on either side of the river.
No one needs me tonight, he sighs to the bartender.

Two lovers inch their way towards the river,
lights out.
All that is left of the moon is a sliver.
Three drunks, on their way home, watch from the riverbank
but they can't decide what to shout:

that a German woman laughs in the fog?
that the bridge has been drinking?
that the wet branches are full of ravens
like black lightbulbs?

a partial foreign policy

The giant sunflower stood guard outside the stucco palace,
thwarting our little revolution.
Its petals hung like a white Amish beard,
its green leaves old and scarred.

My men dozed on their catapults. Marijuana and bees.
Softly the fieldmice relieved them of their crackers.
I steeled myself, accentuating my jaw
in case the scene might be rendered in marble.
Nothing breathed.
Winged flight seemed unusually compelling.
I heard the sap dripping from the trees like a drumroll.

Every morning the gardener on his ladder
took off his shirt and spoke to the sunflower.
He was the key! But my men were too busy
accosting the goats, having worked something out with the goatherd.
Seeing this, I became uncomfortably conscious of the hairs
    on my body,
which are black, though my pompadour is blond.
It occurred to me I will never know what to trust.

cruikshank's rheumy eyes

Cruikshank by the fo'c'sle.
Or the scuttlebutt, engaged in scuttlebutt,
I don't know, I'm new at this. Three days
from the harbormaster's lean wife,
fifteen days from an island
lush, with monkeys.

And how many days to the moon, I ask him.
He has a terrible crooked thigh,
white as a bowel pulled out into the night.

And how many days straight down?
With our cargo of glitzy knickknacks,
less than a day
to settle, to begin the process
of fossilization. For that is where it begins—
worn-out molluscs, cracked bivalves, and kamikazes
piling up in mud. Finger bones of lovers in the dark.

natural disaster

A man and a woman make love
under a canopy of bees.
He holds his arms out to fly,
she mutters the captions of famous paintings.

Outside, the river overflows its banks in the sun.
The land tilled for apples foams up
like a pail of cleanser.

The bees maintain their levitation
through the strictest concentration:
they recite to themselves forest-industry figures.

The flood brings great passion to many people
stranded on their roofs:
they had always wanted to say something
to each other in the office. . . .

The rescue squad has been sniffing gasoline
and playing Euchre all night.
They have the curtains drawn,
the telephone cord snipped,
the radio dismantled.

the girl with the rock always in her pocket

I was surprised to find that the burial chamber was intricately
    decorated
on the inside, in its blackness.
There were designs best suited for my fingertips.
It was a story—though I couldn't find the beginning—
that was familiar to me:
the lovers, the eiderdown, a party, travel.
I had to climb the walls to follow the rest of the story.
In it the lovers kept meeting and parting, they enjoyed
    each other's company
and the company of train conductors.
Farther along the wall they met in the city,
    outside the butcher shop.
Her head was wrapped in blue.
His eyes were the size of a discontinued coin.
I followed them around the walls.
There were dark men smeared with what I assumed was her lipstick,
joyless men carved to look like beer steins.
Priests drugged by Arabs.
Furniture that sighed. Her old car scared of being junked.
I followed the lovers into the farthest corner of the chamber.
It was a typical ending: the man was in her bed
with the sheets pulled to his chin. He was trying to think
of what hadn't already been said.

incensation at the funeral

May the angels lead you into paradise
which is your love affair with the plump old woman.

May the martyrs lead you, joyous couple, into the holy city,

where it is still and the trees touching the dark sky are burdened.
After the rain they are still burdened.

May the Innocents save you a campsite in the woods
    north of the holy city,
with the mist falling from the pines
with the stars' electricity.

May the prophets let you tinker at their toolbenches.
May there be chocolate.
May there be no almonds.

May the diggers have the dirt hidden when we come to the grave.

May the work be made easy for us. May they have the device.
You would love the device.

hotel de l'etoile

The long thin window to the stars holds up the tenement.
The column is bent in thought. The floor underneath the window
cries out when someone stands there to look out at the night,
unless it is the young girl with her lemons.

She watches for skiffs avoiding the stars.
Her feathered brother is on one knee, calling down to the shore.
In his backpack are three goats. He's on the lookout
for shipwrecked sailors, who have been seen
checking into other hotels, who have been seen
spending their dark gold on wine without opening their eyes.

the painted couple

A couple paints themselves like the sky so no one will see them.
In this way they hope to stay in bed all day.
In the evenings, they walk as if invisible.
They are overjoyed.
No eyes to either meet or avoid on the sidewalk,
perhaps perfect solitude at last.

Everyone stares. A couple, naked and painted like the sky,
walk down the street holding hands.
They stop to look in the windows of stores.
They point at the shoes. They point at old beads.
The birds rouse themselves from their roosts
and fly at the couple.
Dozens of drowsy birds moving as one,
diving at the couple painted like the sky.

The postman stares from his left-handed truck
and the tavern proprietor stares from behind his stack of matchbooks
and their friends stare from a passing Volkswagen
and a teacher stares from a copy shop, over the lid of a copier,
and the policeman stares from his flashing car.

The couple who painted themselves like the sky
stand before the magistrate, in clothes.
He is speaking. His mouth opens and closes
under his wig.

Wisps of cirrus clouds slip out from under the man's cuffs;
the Pleiades rise and fall under her dress.

a last look at the mutineers

What can the mutineers hear from the hold?

   The thrum of fingers on drums
   and the popping of fat in the fire
   and the insides of the forest saying All of you, just go away.

What else can they smell besides themselves and the salted meat?

   The oil on the freshly sharpened knives on shore.

.

In the stillness one of the mutineers confesses his love
for the Mother Superior who raised him,

one of them cries for the gull endlessly circling the mast
of the ship,

one of them swallows a poisoned tooth
worn on a chain for just this occasion,

and one of them listens carefully enough to envision
the exact size of each drum.

.

The captain is just the tapping of two heels
on the boards above their heads.

The jury is just the occasional nervous laugh from the rigging,

and as for Fate, they have been listening to the sea for days.

the batteries

A poor tribe, and the land is dry
and their huts are lit at night by red stars.
One of the women finds a crate of batteries
by the river and brings it to the nightly dance.

They have little water but beautifully tuned drums.

At night the men gather to discuss new ways to find water:
palm towers that reach up to the clouds like straws,
a forgotten divining song.
The batteries are ignored, left nestling in their crate.

The women then discover they are beautiful.
They wear them from their ears.
They hang them in doorways like curtains.

They are incorporated into ritual:
young men stash them in their mouths,
young women slip them inside themselves
while the musicians breathe into their thin instruments.
Two batteries are buried together in the center of the village
to prevent something as new and unpredictable as the batteries
    themselves.

the empty locket

Wandering the city like the blind astronomer
carefully turning the pages in his sky chart,
I pass a man on the street corner
handing out fliers.
Around his neck is an empty locket.

If you are in love, he says,
get ready for loss.

The fliers are maps showing the seven vent-shafts to Hell,
one of them just outside town.

On Judgment Day,
he whispers
when he sees my engagement ring,
no one will love you in Hell.
.

Morning has broken like the whip
of a dusty rug shaken from a fire escape.

The dust starts to fall but hangs there, livid.

A young woman is in love with me but we rarely meet,
wandering the city.

Fat things lie stagnant in doorways:
old men, bearded ladies, cantankerous rats.

Boxes, seashells, empty
bottles litter the streets.

I think they hiss as I pass. I think
I lost my map of the city
—the creased map that showed
all the short cuts, secret gardens,
red Xs where she and I kissed briefly.

news of the dead pope

Out of a window musical notes float in single file
past the windbreak of sage-colored trees.

The notes are black with mourning. Black birds
hang in the stillness over the courthouses
and other sacred buildings.

At the lake a child notices the sound as if it were coming
from the ground,
out of a strange nautical cellar nearby.

The news travels quickly on such a clear day,
through the clouds shaped like Valkyries,
the clouds swinging swords.

On the child's screened-in porch a radio lights up.
It is old and made of wood;
nevertheless it rises to the occasion.

The child, who heard everything
including the bankers sobbing in the chapel across the lake,

thought he might play saxophone when he grew up.

the funeral of the despotic madman

The watermelons kept their vigil all night.
By the rainspout nine plump women
rinsed their hands, gummy with clay,
while large black birds
circled the gravesite like fighter planes
lost over an island.

With no regard for morbidity
acrobats performed
death-defying feats
across the sky,
while the mourners walked the casket
up the soft hill in orange light.

The pallbearers lost their shoes.
Automatically, the mourners leaked.
The trained chimps with their pastel violas
warbled from the trees.
Their trainers slept
with the leashes looped around their toes.

In the front, kneeling
alongside the watermelons,
was the medicated son,
with a rash from rubbing his hands.

every which way but the luminous fork

A man drives down the highway in a semi with an orangutan
and a luminous fork.
Each week he and the orangutan run around a different truckstop cafe
like maniacs when the maple syrup kicks in.
They pretend to wrestle with a highway patrolman
and then film this and put it on TV.

Meanwhile, the luminous fork lies patiently
in the glove compartment.

The man promised his son he would use the luminous fork
at the Big Texan Steakhouse,
where you get a free 72-ounce steak if you eat it in one hour.
And the luminous fork had always wanted to see the Cadillac
sculpture garden.
When they get there the cars have been defaced
and have no chrome. The orangutan is sick
from a convenience-store sandwich and the luminous fork
notices for the first time how much hair the orangutan's lost.

"The lullaby of the passing traffic!" the orangutan demands
in his own way.
He is sick all over the dash. The man lets him sleep in the truck,
and takes the fork into the Big Texan, where the decor is garish,
to no one's surprise. His waitress looks concerned
when he takes the fork out of his pocket. She thinks:
it's a plot to cheat on a steak!

When the manager tells him he'll have to leave his fork
outside, the man reaches for his gun.
The manager reaches for his, and they shoot clean,
perfectly round holes in each other,
which awakens the orangutan from a dream
about truckstops.

two

drama

The scene is a mountain road and we pull off at the pyramid.
The forest is old and corrugated with moss.
A stream recites something.

The cast of characters includes my best friend, and a doctor
with Chinese breasts.

To the right of the stage a spinster jabs knitting needles
into her couch.

To the left of the stage a girl serves sushi on tiptoes
over a greasy counter.

The props include plants with seven leaves, the "Largest Hamburger
in the World," and a bottle of wine.

My best friend takes deep breaths. He should be played as if he lives
in Miami.
He should be played in a sailor's suit. He should be played
with serious eyes because he has fled a tropical revolution.

The doctor should be played by a woman with the dark thighs
of a mountaineer.
Her stethoscope is a winged snake napping on her shoulders.
She has plum eyes.

The sun sits mildly over the pyramid with its arms folded
under its chin.

Miles of mountains are humming. The doctor is on call
so she is off-limits. I am relieved to learn this and bend
    to the stream to drink.
She makes me feel gloomy and I am looking forward
to meeting a young painter in August whose breasts they say
are as lonely as a shrimp boat.

a wake for the telephone

An unconnected telephone lies dead on the table.
The cold plastic.
The holes in its earpiece like black, collapsed stars.
The mouthpiece, unable to whine, to recite original poems,
to ask that someone bring over a bottle of wine.

The old couple, eating dinner, were shocked
when the phone threw itself to the floor instead of ringing again,

its spiral cord like the wet hair of a girl left behind in a
     tide pool,
the way it lies in a heap on the table,
its dials stuck between numbers.

It will never be used to phone the president.
It will never help old classmates find each other.
It will no longer suffer the awkward silence while asking
     for a date.
There will be no more heavy breathing.

In many ways the phone is relieved.

conflagration

I wish I could take back every bad thing
I said about the furnace:
Sirens perched in the empty trees
are trying to blow my windows out,
the milk is freezing.

My recurring dream is a postcard
my uncle sent me when I was six:
people leap from burning buildings
into burning grass.

A few rise in beams of light
into the bodies of brooding Saucers:
these people's faces are pained,
as if they'd forgotten their medication.

The old people were nowhere to be seen.
They huddled in cellars with blankets,
thinking of cots
and cheeses strung up with ropes, shivering.

history lesson

We caught a spy on the edge of camp.
It was sundown.
The pigs in their pens howled when we brought him in.
We led him to a pole on the parade ground
and sent for our sons. Sons, we said,
This is what happens.

It was something horrible. I forget. Something
horrible and slow.
Meanwhile, the officers' horses were helpless
to brush off the vampire bats, having, of course,
no hands. . . .

The spy stayed tied to the pole for days.
In the sun he seemed to move occasionally.
But then again, there seemed to be water in the distance.

to a croatian poet

The snow spread-eagled on the ground
muffles the sound of falling bodies.
It seems people are leaping from buildings again
like white petals falling from large trees.

A field worker napping against a trunk is smothered.

Doves descend from on high,
severing the power lines like live snakes on the sidewalk.
A boy in a sailor suit squats to touch. . . .

As you watch, a car comes squealing around the corner.
In your bedroom cupola you instinctively know
it is you they're after.
You barely have time to hide the silver,
to strangle the parrot who has learned
your poems by heart.

Their boots chew up the spiral stairs.
You hear the change jingling in their pockets,
or is that ammunition?
And where is that pistol your grandfather left you
on his deathbed?
Is it under his cassocks,
under the starched rings of his collars?

Now they paw at the door, growling in some other dialect,
some thick tongue spoken across the river.
Saliva from their jaws pools under the door.

The world is ugly and the people are sad,
you say, leaving a last love note for your wife.

how do you explain the matter of love to a house?

The house looks in on itself at sundown.

A man and a woman are making love in the kitchen,
up against the refrigerator.

The house doesn't comprehend this and just sits,
watching what is going on inside itself.

The refrigerator shudders and tries to shrug them off.
The bed is in hysterics: see how funny they are now, it taunts.

The man and woman return to the dining room,
where the sacher torte sits sternly.
It bites its tongue when she cuts the first slice.
It passes out from the pain of his first bite.

It pleads with them from the plate.

The plates tremble too, as the man and woman
run hot water, as they fill
the dishwasher with harsh soap.

ein kleine nacht mischief

The juice we let out of the police cars
spelled complete nonsense on the asphalt
while the passing trucks murmured
with their lowered lids.
The trees had been recast in ice
by someone with a brooding hand.

In extremes, as in a desert or the Bible,
a staff will curl around a hand,
having turned into a deadly asp;
in this case the sergeant's truncheon
wagged below his belt.

The police questioned us separately
without letting us confer.
In the black park they pulled us apart
with the warm car between us.
They thought of new questions with surprising alacrity
and a real feel for precision.
The pond groaned as it froze to death.
Black birds pissed on the frozen trees and they shattered.

The juice we let out of the police cars
froze in a crystalline form
that was irregular and absurd.
The light was brittle and hurt our faces.
There was no need for depressants.
It was so cold it hurt to tell the truth
by which I mean

there were our tender teeth to consider.

letter to hoopy

Hoopy come back it's winter
and the animals are clammy.

Come back someone scratched a triptych on my windowpane at night,
I saw the bears great-grandma killed, in the stars.

Hoopy do you suffer aortal confusion like my tragic dad?

Hoopy was it the guns that scared you?
Or the neighbors crawling out of ditches who were holding them?
Sometimes I want to believe the prairie is like the sea.
No one owns a pickup with a figurehead.
"If great-grandma can climb Buck Mountain so can I," right?
but I never did.

I stayed under the dark elm afraid of the family headstones
even in the sun. The red birds crept
back and forth on the branches above me.

cribbage rules

Two, three, or more players.
Cut the deck to decide on the dealer.
The player with the least offensive hand lays down the first card.
If a player cannot lay down a card without offending the other
    players,
he or she is dismissed.
If a brother and sister are playing they may not be on the
same team, and their discussions must be limited.
Each player pays special attention to one opponent.
A player holding a jack of the same suit as the hostess
is dismissed.
A player who is too fidgety is dismissed.
A player can be dismissed for yawning.

The dealer should pour the drinks.
One player is chosen whose goal is to put the deck back
    the way it was
before it was cut; the opponents may not use nouns when speaking
    to this player.

When each player has used all of his or her cards,
the glasses should be refilled.
The object is to collect all the cards somehow.
This should take place in a darkened room lit only by forks.
Stillness is an important part of the scoring:
the first one to move a finger loses.

from a mosaic found in the basilica

God is a tiger, so the people worship him from the trees.

His cries roll down the hills at dusk and the old people
huddle the children into their beds.
Hopefully, they say, we'll sleep tight tonight.

The sky and the trees are a grainy photograph
after the sun sets and children strike at bats
that flutter under streetlights.

The churches are in the jungle
and the priests are gaunt and white and bless
each other in the basement sacristy secretly
while God paces outside.
Their gray brittle ears prick up at the brush
of His hair along the walls.

Out in the pews, the parishioners
sit nervously on their hands.

The cardinals holed up in the basilica grin,
having thought up Purgatory:
the ultimate fundraiser.

The jugglers are dragged
kicking from their car to be beaten
by priests in their dark frocks.

Drunken saints in jackboots and tunics
pace the floor of the bar after services.

On their breasts are His silver claws.

Think of the proprietor, a quivering pail of water
that stands too close to the electrical outlet.

Try not to think of the clock ticking over the bar.

a short history of illumination

Concerning a nun, composer and herbalist,
and the miracles she concocts on her travels,
at the end of which she is to be investigated.

Aren't all plants sacred, she asks along the way,
especially the poisonous ones?
The tinker under his enormous hat grins
as she hands him the red vial.

In her chamber after midnight
she is engulfed in fire
and after she's put it out by rolling on the tiles
there is a new song in her mouth.

She performs her songs from the tops of steeples.
They are said to bring peace to the village.
Of a woman who wears a smock that was hung out to dry
during this performance, it is said that no man can resist her,
that cats follow her into the bedroom.

Safest to say the nun's songs were given to her by God.
Safest to say, "I should write holy words to this."

Best not to think of the curtain that speaks.
Best not to send down the singed gown.
Best not to admit composing while in flames.

rat

The rat busies himself with his fur, with his neatly stacked
pile of bones. Though you held your breath at night
and lifted the loose eyelash from his cheek you never expected
the love-spell would work. Now you are in his dark basement
with his unavoidable caresses.

Upstairs, along the Ramblas, young people in bright feathers glide.
A gaudy and drunken aesthete wanders by with cathedral blueprints
rolled in his sleeve.

You are bored by opium and everything is dim
and predictable:
rats are collecting bones and scribbling
philosophies on towels.
Sigh: one of them loves you like a comet.

when i cut off my hand

it sat on the counter beside the pans like a flattened pork medallion. Someone poured the wine so the kitchen glimmered with the wine glasses on their slender legs. Outside, a tender snowfall spotted the red roofs. Before the chef could drop his scallions my hand crawled away, weary of my clumsiness. Cut probably fifteen times, missing a knuckle, new wounds crossing old wounds. I lost the knuckle trying to carve charms from green branches over a campfire. In the black canyon beyond the trees I heard large birds arranging piles of bones all night until the depressants kicked in. That was a time of great distress, and the empty necks of bottles pointed up at me from the ground. I thought they were saying Oh, again and again.

Fed up, and free of me, my hand slipped under the kitchen door to begin its new life. And what use was a disenchanted hand to me? A hand with more than one itchy finger? A hand whose new life began at the bus stop across from the hedge maze, in which it stalked a clueless librarian. A hand that pinched a young girl in glasses from under a newspaper on an icy bench. A hand molesting women on their way home from the dentist, a hand pointing at a boy with a twisted leg.

ah yes, that question

The doctors have given up, they are at the reception desk
    whispering
to the old secretaries. The third floor is thick with flowers.
A priest is lost in thought.
He reads the caption of an oil painting.

In each room a patient wheezes.
Their diseases are unknowable; the doctors have given up,
there is a smell that could be their bodies or the food
    they ordered.
Their wheezing joins the throaty fluorescent lights.

The priest, who is not permitted to give up, makes his rounds again.
In the rooms the TV screens are blue and fluid drips bravely.
The doctors have given up, so squat machines watch the patients
and coo consolingly. The patients are shrinking.
A girl and boy are sent from room to room to comfort them
but with the doors closed, she kisses the boy's cheek.
The patients are oblivious and the fluid drips.
The doctors have given up, they have left behind their stethoscopes,
which lie there, listening and listening.

longing's sculpture garden

In the middle of the day the raven
flies lazily through the statues,
changing out of dark underclothes in a tree shaped like an embrace.
And the bees are miniature dirigibles,
and the ants are the hurrying businessmen,
and the grass is all the money to be made.

In the low light of the evening,
the red trees send their whispered desires
down the lanes on the backs of mayflies.
And the trees, with their mile-long trunks, are the Great Books,
and the robin is a widow planting new poppies on a grave.

The night is under the spell of the two marble breasts;
it coils obediently in the trellis.
And the deer who come out are the nervous students,
and the dandelions are lovers who strain to touch each other
    in the wind.

map of lament

oh forces uncontrollable who knock my posters from the walls
oh room that swells in the rain and weeps all night
oh domestic quarrel we can hear next door
oh mischievous wind, which is love's headstone
oh people who carry old letters in their jackets,
who cheer for the grass in the sidewalks

the man with the sooty wings

If I could see water in the bay,
then I would see the shrimp boats hanging their black veils.
If I could see the mailboat steaming away
then I would begin counting the days until you answer
on my fingers, my toes, my curled hairs, the chambers of my heart.

If I could see the mailboat I would see it falter,
hit a reef and sink like an empty bottle.

If only you could see me in my first tuxedo.
If only my wings weren't heavy with soot and unused to my new weight.

I imagine that in your country the people can see each other
and are buying artichokes from stands.

I imagine that you walk the wood floor of your room,
that your simple breasts are heavy,
that you are listening to the news,
which has been reduced to weather and death.

letter in april

The mailman stands at the edge of the cliff
at the seminary, going up and down on his toes.
It is a blustery day; the gray wind rolls
in over the landfill.

He can still see his satchel
on its way towards the sea:
the letters hanging above it.

The burning town casts its shadows
on his back.
People's screams are taken up by the gulls
who are circling, waiting to be fed

by the nervous novice in the garden.
Inside, the lovers are tracing the cosmotesque floors
with their fingers, she is kissing each tile.
In the reliquary a curled hand whispers dark words
they ignore.

the toads, 1975

A boy told me his father had been eaten by toads,
a swarm of toads with foaming mouths and lidless eyes.

The war had just ended
and not everyone was home.
There was a dead pope.
Helicopters still practiced parting trees.

Our neighbor made home movies from his cockpit
and showed them to my father and me.
I liked the sound the popcorn made in my head
while a man on a bicycle hurried to cross
what was surely an unimportant bridge
on a simple river.

The boy's father did lie in a polluted puddle,
toads slept in his pockets,
I learned this later.

the necklace

We knew our father was watching us when his opera glasses flashed in the setting sun. Soon he would come put his arms around us in a way that surely seemed kind but which hurt when he dug his thumbnails into our shoulders.

The first morning of spring at breakfast, with a light tap of the spoon on the egg in his egg cup, he told us no one was allowed to touch the honeysuckles anymore. They were poison and furthermore they were sacred and they were God's as well and not ours, though they grew in our backyard.

All spring we lay under them envying the hummingbird. All spring we made up words for the smell. We made up a secret for the honeysuckle and whispered it to our dog.

On the morning of the Solstice the young woman who came to teach us our lessons plucked a flower from the honeysuckle and drew the stem out from the bottom and touched the honey to her tongue. She did not die so we ran outside, pulling the flowers, lining them up: lest to most exquisite. We planned to string them into a necklace for her.

It grew hot. It grew more difficult to remember which end of the long line of honeysuckle blossoms was better. We each had one in our hands so we tried them again.

They tasted good, in fact they all tasted the same and we held them between our fingers and the opera glasses flashed in the window and the young woman walked through the gate into the street though she hadn't taught us our lessons for the day.

a young person's guide to the month of june

When your day begins with a distinct awareness of your own death
    inspired by a television theme song you woke up with
    in your head

and when at work you are only able to produce long lists
    of questions,
    thoughtful questions, insightful questions, pages
    of unanswerable
    questions splintering off like the family tree

and when for lunch you drive through town and people you don't know
    wave at you from shop windows where they are hanging flags

and when the evening is too humid for lovers to lie together
    but they do it anyway and later regret the arousal on the
    clinging sheets

and when, and especially when, your lover is gone
    and you stay awake for an hour scratching mosquito bites
    on your thighs

and when the neighborhood is tense because of what happened to that
    little girl, so tense that a door slamming sets off car alarms and
    incites the animals

and when on a Sunday old men are seen weeping at the corner bar
    because they have lost track of their sons or their sons
    are childbeaters and it is Father's Day

and when the heat is too much for certain birds who fall right
    out of the sky

then be patient.

quick sell the pig

All sorts of plants were beautiful
and seemed worthy of description.
The trees, for instance, fingered low clouds suggestively.
Construction awaited an impressive building.
Teachers led their classes to the flowerbeds,
to write in their notebooks.
One particular flower—the rose—
attracted the most attention.
They wrote "It is very red"
then chased the girl who smelled.
From an open window: timpani.
From a passing car: a thin rainbow on the damp streets.
From the farms outside town: the unmistakable smell.
The fog rolled down every street alphabetically,
while small groups of people strolled by the river
pretending to listen to each other.
One man worried he would be asked which part of dusk
he liked best.
The part at the beginning when the bats come out
and everything seems possible,
or the part at the end when all that can be seen
in the moon is bright mud.

will the red hand throw me?

1.

Though our radiator is painted the color of the walls
we know he's there. Whatever we set on top of him
bursts angrily into flame.
He has come to be known as Petulant.
He has come to be known as Wasted Space.
To be contrary, the radiator will not heat us when we need it.

"If only I could find his fucking face,"
I say to her (who sleeps beside me),
"I'd stick something in his eye. I'd stick this in his eye."
And I hold out a fork. Night has grown up around us
and this luminous fork is our only light.

2.

By the light of our luminous fork I see
the old Mexican shortwave radio weeping in the corner.
All her tubes are cracked and it is late in the century.
No one will be putting on a hat and boots
to find tubes for her, because they can't be found.

She is like the last auk in its cage
with a shattered wishbone,
while the naturalists were helpless and could only offer
to bring it something, again and again.
She is like the last passenger pigeon when it realized it was
     the last passenger pigeon.

We don't notice her anymore.
"God's curse on you for ignoring me," she used to moan at night.
Now she only weeps or says her prayers,

but either way we can't hear her because her tubes are withered
and it is late in the century.

3.
The luminous fork is also worthy of investigation:

Our grandparents cannot remember when the luminous fork first came
    into their lives.
It was prefigured by the tools of Poseidon and Michael.
It has appeared in my poems before.
It is the last of the luminous flatware and is lonely
in our drawer.
Imagine a luminous fork in the company of our silverware
and their steely glances.
Think about this fork who cannot share his secrets
    with the dark knives,
who will never lie with the smooth spoons.

The luminous fork knows that someday when I open the drawer
I won't recognize him among the tarnished forks pointing at me,

just as I am told one day there will come a knock at my door
that I won't answer.

found in the museum of old science

Beyond the sky is a great river, along whose banks grow spectacular plants: the celestial peach, the moon rose, the lily-of-the-void. When the flowers fall into the river and sink to the bottom, the river overflows and a drop of water is forced out of the bottom into the sky. Finding itself all alone up there, it falls.

Unlike snowflakes, there are only three types of raindrops.

A raindrop crowded out by a celestial peach blossom is the largest and falls the fastest. A raindrop crowded out by a moon rose falls at an angle and is nearly impossible to catch on the tongue. A raindrop crowded out by the lily can fall through the eye of a needle, if you hold it just right.

Unlike a tear, a raindrop has no parents. A raindrop has no idea why it has been born, and sadly, no one to ask. So one does not hear raindrops complain when they fall onto the clear roof of a greenhouse.

As a raindrop falls it reflects the whole world. A raindrop falling over Oklahoma seems evenly divided by roads. A raindrop falling onto a grove of aspens in a pine forest seems to have left its lights on. A raindrop falling on one city holds a knife; on another, a tiny black pistol. A raindrop falling into your eye think it's you, watching a raindrop fall into its eye.

Famous Raindrops:

Obviously, the first one to fall.
The lucky raindrop who fell down the neck of Helen's dress.
The drop that tried to save the library at Alexandria.
The first raindrop to land on the Ark, on the nose of the figurehead that was Noah's wife.
Edison's favorite raindrop; the one he kept in a test tube.
The last drop Beethoven ever heard.

mandrake

Mandrake, which shrieks when pulled from the ground,
    especially at dusk.
Mandrake, from which a narcotic is prepared.
Mandrake, whose root is the shape of a man, though a small man,
    easily overlooked among the faces at nightfall.
Small man, easily overlooked, who was hanged at the crossroads.
His thin neck which snapped, causing an erection.
His semen which fell into the clover beside certain old women.
Certain old women who have not maried and are under suspicion
    by the police, who stare into their houses with opera glasses.
The sickly ghost of the small man wandering the backroads because
    the police hanged him at the crossroads to confuse his ghost.
The police, whose superstitions were well-founded and sleep peacefully
    because the ghost has wandered into the next village.
Certain old women in the next village who have met with the women
    in the first village at the crossroads between the two.
Mandrake, from which a narcotic is prepared, shrieking as the women
    pull it from the clover.
The roots in the shape of little pale men between the women's fingers
    under the new moon.
The stockpot which has been boiling for weeks.
The little pale roots thrown in.
The narcotic, which boils for weeks, and which the women drink
    before a town meeting.
Their pronouncements in a language they do not speak.
The gift of True Vision, which the narcotic gives them, though
    in the two days they are affected they do not notice
    anything different than it was.
The realization that nothing is different than it was.

The despair that overcomes the women, especially when they learn
    from the small man's ghost that the police mean to hang them
    at the crossroads.
The shrieks of the mandrake being pulled from the clover
    near the women's hanging feet three days later by the police
    who want to put a stop to the narcotic.
The rumor that during a new moon at the crossroads the ghosts
of certain women will lead you to a stockpot
    which has been boiling for weeks,
    where the gift of True Vision awaits you, you who are so eager
    to see all there is to see.

a hummock in the malookas

<u>for Jennifer Kitchell</u>

From a hummock in the Malookas
I have a clear view of heaven.

It is the stars pinpricking the grass
through a hole.

It is the blue snow we awaken to.

From a hummock in the Malookas,
where the women run topless
until they have worn a dirt path around
the island, I have a clear view of heaven.

It is the glidepaths of satellites blinking over pizzerias.

It is the spindly Southern Cross I have yet to see.

It is our nearest star anointing
the heads of all the flowers equally
and the green roofs of terrariums.